Published by Creative Education
P.O. Box 227, Mankato, Minnesota 56002
Creative Education is an imprint of The Creative Company
www.thecreativecompany.us

Design by Stephanie Blumenthal
Production by Christine Vanderbeek
Art direction by Rita Marshall
Printed in the United States of America

Photographs by Alamy (North Wind Picture Archives, Photos 12, The Print
Collector), Corbis (Bettmann, Christie's Images, Jim Erickson, Jeremy Horner),
Getty Images (Joseph H. Baily/National Geographic, Dorling Kindersley, French
School, Hulton Archive, MPI, NYPL/Science Source, Eugenio Lucas y Padilla,
Spanish School, Universal History Archive, Newell Convers Wyeth), Superstock
(The Art Archive, Everett Collection, Image Asset Management Ltd., Newberry
Library, Pantheon, Photri Images)

Library of Congress Cataloging-in-Publication Data
Gunderson, Jessica.
Conquistadors / by Jessica Gunderson.
p. cm. — (Fearsome fighters)
Summary: A compelling look at conquistadors, including how and why they
sailed to the New World, their lifestyle, their weapons, and how they remain
a part of today's culture through books and film.
Includes bibliographical references and index.
ISBN 978-1-60818-183-4
1. Soldiers—Spain—History—Juvenile literature. 2. Military art and science—
History—Juvenile literature. [1. America—Discovery and exploration—
Spanish—Juvenile literature.] I. Title.

E123.G86 2011
970.01'50922—dc23   2011035799

First edition
2 4 6 8 9 7 5 3 1

CONQUISTADORS

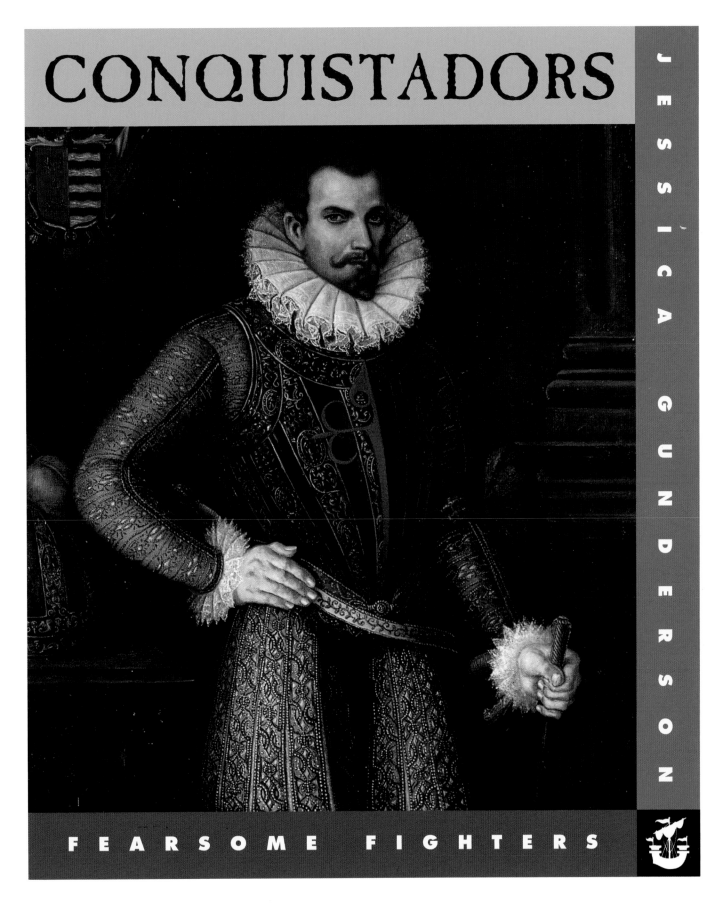

JESSICA GUNDERSON

FEARSOME FIGHTERS

CREATIVE EDUCATION

From the beginning of time, wherever groups of people have lived together, they have also fought among themselves. Some have fought for control of basic necessities—food, water, and shelter—or territory. Others have been spurred to fight by religious differences. Still others have fought solely for sport. Throughout the ages, some fighters have taken up arms willingly; others have been forced into battle. For all, however, the ultimate goal has always been victory.

After the European discovery of the Americas in 1492, Spanish conquistadors (a word that means "conquerors") set off for the "New World," conquering land for their country. Armed with guns, cannons, and swords, the conquistadors ravaged the land and its people as they dreamed of finding legendary cities of gold. For more than 50 years, these men tromped through unexplored territory seeking riches, killing or enslaving all who got in their way—feats that were lauded by Europeans and inspired fear in the American natives. Successfully **colonizing** many parts of North and South America, these men changed the course of world history. Although the days of the conquistadors ended long ago, their fascinating stories of greed, rivalry, and destruction are still told today.

THE QUEST FOR GOLD

The Spanish conquistadors rose to glory by conquering the Americas in the 16th century. In the preceding centuries, Spain was in a constant state of tumult, divided into the four major kingdoms of Castile, Aragon, Navarre, and Granada, and undergoing repeated invasions by the Moors, **Muslims** from North Africa. Since 711, the region's Christians had been trying to drive the Moors from their lands. The warring went on until the late 1400s, when the Moors were driven from all but the region of Granada in southern Spain.

In 1469, Princess Isabella of Castile (1451–1504) married Prince Ferdinand of Aragon (1452–1516), which united the two kingdoms and later created the kingdom of Spain. When they became king and queen, the couple pledged to rule together equally. One of their major goals was to unite the remaining Spanish kingdoms and to fully expel the Moors

from Granada. In 1492, Granada finally came under the control of the Spanish Christians, and in 1512, Queen Isabella I and King Ferdinand II gained control of Navarre. Spain was united.

In 1486, an Italian explorer named Christopher Columbus (1451–1506) had approached Isabella and Ferdinand with a plan. He wanted to sail westward in search of a new route to the East Indies, islands off the coast of Asia. In the 1480s, much trade was done between Europe and Asia, but merchant ships had to sail south around the Cape of Good Hope, the southern tip of Africa, to reach Asia. No one had tried sailing west, and no one suspected that an entire continent lay between Europe and Asia. With funding from the king and queen, Columbus set sail in 1492, landing upon the island of Hispaniola (present-day Haiti and the Dominican Republic) 10 weeks later. The island was inhabited by people whom

CARRYING THE BANNER OF SPAIN, CHRISTOPHER COLUMBUS CHANGED THE "NEW WORLD" FOREVER WITH HIS LANDING

Columbus called Indians, believing he'd landed in the East Indies.

Columbus sailed back to Spain to tell Isabella and Ferdinand about his discovery. The royals, sensing that Columbus had found lands previously unknown, realized the potential of settling this new world. Claiming these lands for Spain would enable them to establish an **empire** and to become the most powerful **monarchs** in Europe. They sent Columbus back to Hispaniola, where he and the soldiers accompanying him were soon killing and enslaving the "Indians" and creating a Spanish colony—becoming, in effect, the first of the Spanish conquistadors. By 1515, about 80 percent of the native population of Hispaniola had died, either at the hands of the Spaniards or from European diseases such as smallpox. The rest were enslaved and forced to pan for gold or labor on sugar cane plantations.

As the Spanish began settling Hispaniola and the neighboring island of Cuba, they heard stories about great civilizations of the vastly unexplored land to the west (present-day Central and North America). The civilizations of native peoples such as the Mayas and the Aztecs were rumored to have cities of pure gold. One story told of a king named El Dorado who bathed each morning in gold dust and had a kingdom of pure-gold buildings and streets. Another tanta-

Columbus's interactions with America's natives were initially friendly, but that soon changed

FERDINAN. MAGALA.

The Spanish discovery of the Americas launched what became known as the Age of Discovery. From the 15th through the 17th centuries, Europeans explored the globe in search of new trading partners, goods, and trade routes. They charted new lands and waters and laid claim for their countries. The English, French, and Dutch surveyed many parts of North America and established colonies there. Others searched for water routes to the Pacific. One famous voyage was that of Ferdinand Magellan (1480–1521) of Portugal, who led the first expedition to sail around the world. Although he died before it was completed, Magellan's journey gave Europeans wider knowledge of Earth's geography.

CONQUISTADORS

lizing tale concerned the Seven Cities of Gold, which stemmed from a centuries-old story of seven monks who left Europe and founded cities of wealth and splendor. Such stories unleashed a hunger for gold across Spain, luring the adventurous men who would become known as conquistadors to travel far and wide in search of riches. Even as the existence of such golden places became more and more improbable, the conquistadors lusted for wealth and continued to search. "With gold," said Columbus, "one may do what one wishes in the world."

Although gold was the primary motivator, the conquistadors were also driven by God and glory. Isabella and Ferdinand, fervent Catholics, desired to spread Christianity (specifically Catholicism) throughout the world. Although the **indigenous** people of the Americas were very religious, they were not Christian and thus deemed **heathens**. They practiced rituals such as worshiping the sun and offering human sacrifices. The Spanish had never seen such rituals and viewed them as strange and barbaric. The

indigenous people needed to be "saved" by the word of God, Isabella and Ferdinand thought, and they ordered that priests accompany the conquistadors on their expeditions. As they trekked through the Americas, the conquistadors demanded that the natives accept Christianity and pledge allegiance to Spain. Those who did were sometimes spared the wrath of the conquistadors and allowed to keep their land and wealth. More often than not, the conquistadors killed or enslaved them anyway.

The conquistadors who traveled to the New World in search of fame and fortune were brazen and brave. Stopping at nothing to achieve success, small Spanish armies led by conquistador officers took on indigenous forces that sometimes outnumbered them by tens of thousands. Often funding their own expeditions, conquistadors claimed the land they conquered in the name of Spain and declared themselves local rulers. Under the *encomienda* system, successful conquistador soldiers were granted swaths of land by Spain as well as ownership of all people

After the unification of Spain, Queen Isabella and King Ferdinand sought to foster national unity under one form of Christianity—Catholicism. In 1478, they established a tribunal, or governmental panel, called the Spanish Inquisition, which punished or banished those who were not Roman Catholic, citing heresy. Even many of those who had outwardly converted to Catholicism, such as the country's many Jews and Muslims, were suspected of practicing their religions secretly and were brought to trial and sentenced. Many suffered torture or death, and an estimated 3,000 were burned at the stake. Although such brutal methods were eventually abandoned, the Inquisition continued to imprison and punish non-Catholics for three centuries, not officially ending until 1834.

upon it. Each report of a new conquest inspired others to launch their own expeditions.

Some conquistadors who had served in other conquistador armies now desired fame for themselves. Hernán Cortés (1485–1547), who had served in the conquest of Cuba, was one of the first conquistadors. In 1519, he led an expedition into present-day Mexico, taking on the Aztecs and ultimately destroying their way of life. Inspired by Cortés's success, Francisco

Pizarro (c. 1475–1541), who in 1513 had crossed the Isthmus of Panama—the narrow strip of land in Central America that lies between the Caribbean Sea and the Pacific Ocean—with another famed explorer, Vasco Nuñez de Balboa (c. 1475–1519), conquered the Incas in present-day Peru. Hernando de Soto (c. 1496–1542), who had served with Pizarro, explored what is now the southeastern United States in the early 1540s, while at the same time Francisco Vásquez

---

THE CONQUISTADORS' EXPLORATIONS CONTRIBUTED GREATLY TO THE SLOWLY FORMED MAPS OF THE TWO AMERICAN CONTINENTS

CONQUISTADORS

de Coronado (1510–54) was journeying through the southwestern U.S. in search of the Seven Cities of Gold.

Although Portugal, France, England, and Holland also sent explorers to the New World, the Spanish were quick to claim lands as their own, stifling settlement by other Europeans, especially in Central and South America. The conquistadors sent gold and other riches back to Spain, and with each new conquest, Spain became wealthier and more powerful. The decimation of the indigenous populations was scarcely given a thought as the golden age of Spanish exploration approached its zenith. Columbus had opened the door to the Americas, and the conquistadors sailed boldly through.

HAVE WEAPONS, WILL CONQUER

The formidable weapons the conquistadors carried helped them succeed against the native armies they encountered in the Americas. Conquistador foot soldiers charged into the midst of indigenous armies with guns blasting, the loud bang and flash more fearsome than the actual damage caused. The most popular gun was the harquebus. Invented in Spain in the mid-1400s, the harquebus had an S-shaped arm called a serpentine that was attached to the barrel. When it was time to fire, the conquistador would clamp a burning piece of rope, called a matchlock, into the jaws of the serpentine. A pull of the trigger would drop the serpentine into the barrel, where the burning rope would ignite the gunpowder and release the projectile, usually an iron ball. Early harquebuses were so unwieldy and heavy that the end of the barrel needed a forked rest to support it, and shots were not very accurate, even by the most practiced of shooters.

The harquebus also took time to load, light, and reload, making it not the most practical of weapons in a fierce battle.

Conquistador **infantry** used the crossbow—a bow mounted crosswise on a stock or support—just as much as the harquebus. Although also unwieldy, the crossbow needed less maintenance than the harquebus, especially in the humid climate of the Americas. The crossbow also had a more accurate aim, launching projectiles called bolts, which were smaller and heavier than arrows. A crossbow bolt could travel as far as 500 yards (457 m), but for reliable accuracy, the target usually needed to be within a range of about 40 yards (37 m).

The preferred weapon of the conquistadors was the rapier, a thin, sharp sword forged in Toledo, Spain. In the 15th century, Toledo sword crafters adopted new techniques from the Moors for tempering metal. These new techniques of

---

MOUNTED AND WELL-ARMED, THE CONQUISTADORS HAD A DECISIVE FIGHTING ADVANTAGE OVER THEIR NATIVE FOES

using hard steel to give a sword strength and soft steel to give it flexibility allowed for a rapier that was lighter, sharper, and narrower than earlier swords but just as strong. A rapier's hilt had metal rings that could be used to catch an opponent's sword and disarm him. Designed for European warfare, the rapier was thin enough to slip through gaps in body armor and sharp enough to pierce **chain mail**, and it was effective against the indigenous warriors of the Americas as well, who wore only light armor made of woven cloth.

The broadsword and halberd were two other popular weapons among conquistadors. At a length of more than three feet (.9 m), a broadsword typically had to be held with two hands. Conquistador **cavalry** would often ride into a fight gripping a broadsword, slashing at densely packed masses of native infantry. The halberd, meanwhile, had a long wooden handle topped by a steel blade that was part ax, part spear point. A soldier could either stab his opponent with the point or swing the ax portion back and forth with two hands, mowing down anyone in his path.

Conquistador armies wheeled cannons called falconets across the land. The falconet had a range of more than 2,000 yards (1,829 m) and could kill or wound multiple men with a single blast. Falconets were often mounted on the rails of ships, and the conquistadors adapted them for war in inland America by building makeshift wheeled carriages for the cannons and pulling them with horses.

Although portraits of famous conquistadors commonly show them in heavy, decorated armor, most conquistadors likely did not wear such armor on the battlefield. A full suit of solid plate armor, consisting of several pieces that covered the shins, thighs, chest, arms, and shoulders, was popular in European medieval warfare but impractical in the Americas. Body armor was heavy and trapped a lot of heat, which would have been uncomfortable in the hot, tropical climates of the New World. High humidity, common in the Americas, would have caused armor to rust, forcing the conquistadors to clean or paint it regularly. Also, such heavy armor was unnecessary, for the native populations used mostly wooden or stone weapons rather than metal ones. While hand-held native weapons, such as the club and the glass-edged wooden sword, were still dangerous, Spanish soldiers didn't need full suits of heavy armor to protect

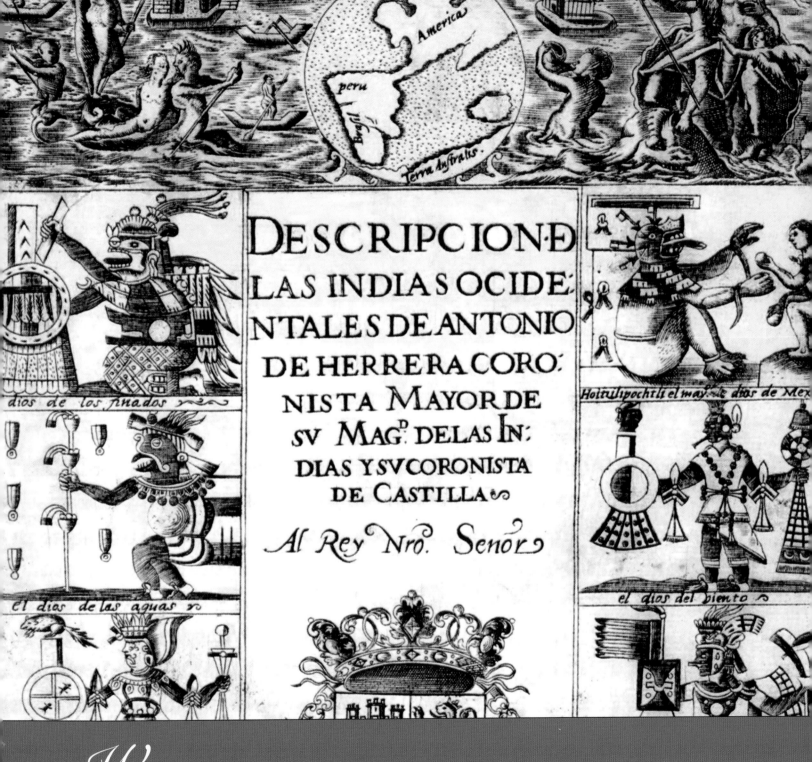

DESCRIPCION D LAS INDIAS OCIDE=NTALES DE ANTONIO DE HERRERA CORO: NISTA MAYOR DE SV MAG.D DELAS IN: DIAS Y SV CORONISTA DE CASTILLA

Al Rey Nrō. Señor

dios de los finados

el dios de las aguas

Hottilipochtli el may..e dios de Mex

el dios del viento

With German printer Johannes Gutenberg's (c. 1398–1468) invention of the printing press in 1439, which could print books and newspapers in mass quantities, **literacy** became more widespread across Europe. Spanish conquistadors, on their way to the New World, read aloud adventurous tales such as Amadis de Gaula, *a Spanish romance about a fearless, adventurous knight. Other tales featured fabulous kingdoms with names such as Amazon, California, and Patagonia. Some believed these tales were based in truth. Impressed and inspired by such stories about adventure, gold, and kings, the conquistadors often named their conquests after places or people in the fictional tales.*

CONQUISTADORS

them from such an onslaught. It is likely the conquistador armies carried armor with them on expeditions but put it on only for certain planned battles or attacks.

In place of the heavy European armor, conquistadors often adapted clothing and war attire from the native populations. The soldiers in Cortés's army, for example, wore the Aztec *xicolli*, a fringed jacket, and the *tilmatli*, a woven poncho. For armor, they wore cotton-stuffed shirts called *ichcahuipilli*. Woven in thick squares and then soaked in salty water for hardening, the ichcahuipilli could absorb the impact of an arrow, a common weapon of the natives. The native weapons were often projectiles—slings, bows and arrows, and wooden spears—so conquistadors carried shields to deflect them. These shields were typically rounded and made of iron or wood, though they could also be heart-shaped, Moorish-style shields covered in leather.

On their heads, conquistadors wore *chapel de fer*—iron helmets with a round brim and low crown. For extra protection, some soldiers may have worn the sallet, a helmet developed in the 15th century that covered much of the face and contained eye slits. In the 1540s, the morion, a crested helmet with a brim that curved over the ears and rose to a high peak at the front and back of the head, became widely used in the Spanish conquistador expeditions.

Depending on the area the Spaniards wished to conquer, they traveled either by ship or on foot. A common ship of the conquistadors was the caravel. Inspired by the Moors and developed by the Portuguese, the caravel had two or three masts and triangular **rigging** that helped it to sail both with and against the wind. A triangular-rigged vessel is more maneuverable than a square-rigged vessel, and the caravel's small size, typically about 82 feet (25 m) long, allowed conquistadors to sail quickly in and out of the shallow **straits** and inlets of the New World's coasts and islands.

When advancing inland on foot, the conquistadors used horses to help carry their loads. The horses were transported to the New World on ships using a system of harnesses and slings to hold them still without injuring them. Conquistadors often chose sturdy, strong horses that could withstand the varied climates and rough terrain of the Americas. The conquistadors usually didn't travel on established roads and often had to forge single-file through the wilderness on small paths, walking their horses. Battling wind and rain and sometimes snow, the explorers hacked through thick forests and undergrowth with their swords.

he most lethal and feared weapon of the natives was the atlatl, *a throwing device about 18 inches (46 cm) long. Although commonly associated with Aztecs, the atlatl was used by tribes throughout the Americas. The atlatl had a wooden handle and a groove into which a warrior inserted a spear, effectively adding length to his throwing arm. With an overhand motion, the fighter would bring the atlatl forward, releasing the spear with greater velocity and momentum than hand-throwing allowed. One major advantage of the weapon was that it could be handled with just one hand, whereas the bow and arrow required two.*

BATTLING IN THE AMERICAS

During the age of the conquistadors, it was a European gentleman's duty to be a fighter. In western European countries such as England, France, Germany, and Spain, battles were considered to be almost like sporting events. Every **nobleman** had to learn to ride a horse and handle weapons such as swords and lances, but many did not become very skilled. After battle, these men would return to their large estates and live a life of luxury. The common man was not allowed to carry a weapon, which enabled the nobility to retain power in their respective kingdoms and communities. But as Spain became involved in wars against the Moors as well as against the French in Italy, the Spanish army became an army like no other in Europe. Ferdinand and Isabella recruited common citizens to become soldiers and join the army. Many of these soldiers turned war into their careers, training and fighting with a fierce intensity. The new, professional Spanish soldier became the most fearsome fighter in all of Europe, and Ferdinand and Isabella again went against tradition by appointing the best, rather than the richest, to become commanders.

Many soldiers who joined conquistador expeditions were veterans of the wars against the Moors or the French. After these wars had been won or stalled, combat-hardened soldiers enthusiastically accepted the challenge to explore, conquer, and settle the New World. Because they were used to success on the European battlefield, the Spanish conquistadors entered each situation with aggressive confidence. When coming upon an enemy or unknown group of people,

---

QUEEN ISABELLA I AND KING FERDINAND II (ABOVE) REAPED THE BENEFITS OF SPANISH PILLAGING ON DISTANT SHORES

*Malinalli, also called La Malinche by the Spanish, was a woman from the Mexican Nahua tribe who became a slave, mistress, and translator for Hernán Cortés. As a young girl, she had been enslaved by a Mayan tribe, and after Cortés defeated the Mayas in battle, she was given to Cortés and traveled with him to Tenochtitlan. She spoke both Nahuatl and Mayas, and her translating services helped Cortés communicate with native tribes and convince them to join his expedition. The couple had a son named Martín, who was one of the first **mestizos** born in the New World. Some people today view Malinalli as a traitor to the indigenous people, while others honor her as mother of the Mexican race.*

CORTÉS AND MALINALLI

their first reaction was usually to advance with force rather than negotiate. Cortés, for example, fired unprovoked upon the city of Cholula in present-day Mexico, perhaps hoping that news of a quick and brazen victory would find its way to the Aztec capital of Tenochtitlan and strike fear into its people. Such arrogance about his superiority allowed the conquistador to strike against a much larger indigenous army without fear.

The native warriors were often scared of the Spaniards, and the conquistadors took advantage of this fear. Indigenous peoples of the Americas had never seen horses before, and when they first glimpsed the conquistadors atop their horses, some thought the soldiers were half-human, half-beast. Guns and **artillery** were also new to the indigenous people, and the fiery blasts from the guns and the thunderous bellows from the cannons terrified the natives. Some believed that these white men in their midst were really gods with supernatural powers. It was only after the natives became accustomed to such shows of weaponry and realized their attackers were mortal humans that this fear began to wear off.

Many of the native cultures in the Americas had a strong sense of honor, honesty, and fairness. The conquistadors, on the other hand, were not averse to using deception to achieve their goals. The conquistadors took advantage of the natives' sense of honor, often lying to them about their **alliances** or plans. The Spaniards also used hostage-taking as a means of

THE TLAXCALANS BECAME LOYAL ALLIES OF THE SPANIARDS

compelling the native armies to surrender or give them gold. Cortés, Balboa, and Pizarro all captured native kings in order to coerce the indigenous people into surrendering or supplying them with riches.

Without help from the natives, the conquistadors may never have become conquerors. To strengthen their own armies, the Spanish built alliances with natives. As Cortés marched toward Tenochtitlan to defeat the Aztecs, he made alliances with native groups who had themselves been conquered by the Aztecs, such as the Tlaxcalans. Historical accounts suggest that often those who allied with the conquistadors did so under threat; many were afraid of being slaughtered if they did not join with the foreigners. In addition, a large number of natives who were part of the conquistador expeditions were slaves captured in earlier conquests. Native women, too, played a role in the success of the conquistadors. Conquered tribes often surrendered women to the conquistadors, and many became mistresses and helped feed the armies. Without these slaves and warriors acting as guides, laborers, and interpreters, the conquistadors would likely have lost their way, starved, or died as they attempted to navigate strange lands.

Conquistador leaders greatly admired Spanish general Gonzalo Fernández de Córdoba (1453–1515) and emulated his military tactics. Fernández, known as *El Gran Capitán* ("The Great Captain"), led campaigns against the French in the Italian Wars, a series of conflicts between 1494 and 1559. He organized his troops into sections of infantry, cavalry, and artillery. This organizational method allowed the sections to work independently if necessary during battle. He further organized the infantry into what became known as *tercio* (unit of three)—pikemen, swordsmen, and gunners, each specializing in their given weapon. In this way, soldiers were allowed to become experts in a particular aspect of battle. The conquistadors adopted this system when waging battles against the indigenous warriors of the Americas, using crossbowmen, swordsmen, and gunners.

The gun and the crossbow were used in equal measure during battles. Guns could do considerable damage to an enemy, but they took time to prepare and light. While gunners were reloading their weapons, crossbowmen would provide cover, keeping the enemy at bay. Swordsmen,

*The New World offered more than just gold to the Spanish. Spain gained great wealth through the trading of other New World **commodities** such as silver, tobacco, and cacao seeds. The Spanish also introduced new foods to Europe such as chili peppers, corn, and tomatoes, first grown in the New World. The Spanish expanded their wealth by establishing sugar cane plantations, especially in the Caribbean islands, as well as cotton plantations. Spain's colonization of the Americas in the 16th century made it the richest country in the world.*

yeqtla ti tetzavitl
yn mal ques.

meanwhile, stabbed any native warriors who broke through their ranks. After the initial clash of armies, cannons could be positioned to hold off the indigenous fighters.

During battle, the horse provided a significant advantage to the conquistadors. A mounted conquistador could strike downward from a considerable height and was less accessible to a foot soldier. The horse could also be used as a weapon to knock down the enemy. Mobility was key to the conquistador's success. With horses, the Spaniards could move faster, advancing upon the enemy at quick speeds. They could also traverse more easily over rough terrain, such as jungles or mountains, and a soldier on horseback would not tire as quickly as a soldier on foot.

Conquistadors were fierce and often ruthless when a battle was joined, but their military skills and confidence were not the only reasons they were able to conquer the New World. They'd brought mighty weapons, but they'd also brought a silent killer: disease. Native populations had never been exposed to European diseases and had no immunity against them. The most devastating was smallpox, which swept the American continents, eventually killing hundreds of thousands. Many native farmers died, causing a shortage of food that led to widespread famine. Populations weakened by sickness and hunger were no match for the Spanish conquistadors.

THE AZTECS WERE ATTACKED BY THE CONQUISTADORS AND TLAXCALANS (ABOVE) AS WELL AS BY SMALLPOX (OPPOSITE)

THE BOLD, RUTHLESS, AND TRIUMPHANT

The appalling and violent ways in which the ambitious conquistadors conquered the Americas earned them renown in Spain. Being outnumbered by the natives yet still managing to annihilate them made them heroes in their time. Their conquest of the Americas changed the world, and stories of their feats were passed down from generation to generation.

Hernán Cortés was the most notorious of the conquistadors and has been credited with single-handedly destroying an entire civilization. Although this is not entirely true, his legacy is the most remembered—and, to many, the most despised—of all the Spaniards who came to claim land and gold from the native people. Born the son of a **hidalgo**, Cortés traveled to Hispaniola in 1504 in search of wealth, fame, and power. When he heard rumors of Mayan gold, Cortés began planning an expedition to the mainland (present-day Mexico). Although the Spanish governor of

Cuba, Diego Velázquez de Cuellar (1465–1524), tried to stop him, Cortés gathered 500 soldiers and set sail in February 1519 with a fleet of 11 ships to the island of Cozumel, where he met Mayan leaders who told him of the Aztec empire and a glittering city of gold called Tenochtitlan. Cortés and his men sailed to the coast and began journeying inland.

Through pouring rain and over rugged mountains, the conquistadors marched almost 250 miles (402 km) toward the great city. The journey was not a peaceful one. Cortés engaged in battle with native populations, defeating some and convincing others, such as nearly 3,000 Tlaxcalans who resented the Aztecs' power in the region, to join the expedition. In November, Cortés and his warriors came upon Tenochtitlan, a lake island city of grand towers and temples. One of Cortés's warriors, Bernal Diaz del Castillo (1495–1584), later wrote that the city was so

HERNÁN CORTÉS WAS AMONG THE MOST AMBITIOUS CONQUISTADORS, CONQUERING MUCH OF WHAT IS TODAY MEXICO

Not all conquistadors waged war against native Americans. Álvar Nuñez Cabeza de Vaca (c. 1490–c. 1559), who was shipwrecked off the coast of present-day Texas, relied upon the indigenous people to survive. He, along with three other survivors of the disaster, trekked across the northern plains of Mexico and the southern United States, becoming part of the first expedition to cross the North American continent. He wrote detailed descriptions of his journey and the civilizations he encountered. When he later became governor of the Spanish colony in Paraguay, he spoke out against brutalizing and enslaving the natives, for which he was sent back to Spain. He died there in poverty.

beautiful it was like a dream. Cortés was greeted by Montezuma II (c. 1466–1520), the Aztec king. Montezuma and many of his people believed Cortés was an ancient god who had come back to claim the Aztec Empire, and Cortés did not correct them. Taking advantage of the king's hospitality, he imprisoned Montezuma, and when Cortés heard that another Spanish conquistador was coming to arrest him for defying Velázquez's orders, he left Tenochtitlan in charge of another captain. While he was gone, however, the captain launched attacks on native citizens who were gathered at a festival, and the Aztecs struck back. Cortés returned to find his men under siege, and, after Montezuma was killed (possibly by accidental fire from his own people), Cortés and his warriors escaped in the dead of night.

Cortés had to make a plan. Because Tenochtitlan was on a lake island, he needed to attack by water. He forced 8,000 of his native companions to build ships, and then he and his warriors sailed to the city and began fighting street by street, killing anyone in their path. After 80 days of battle, during which nearly 100,000 indigenous people were killed, the Aztecs surrendered. Tenochtitlan, now in ruins, was Cortés's possession. He became leader of the new Spanish colony, which was called New Spain, and enslaved many of the native people. However, gold was not as abundant as the rumors had suggested, and Cortés was left to believe that the Aztecs had hidden the precious metals somewhere else.

THIS ILLUSTRATION SHOWS TENOCHTITLAN AS IT LOOKED WHEN THE CONQUISTADORS CAME UPON IT IN THE 1500S

CONQUISTADORS

Although Cortés is widely considered the most ruthless of the conquistadors, his legacy is rivaled by Francisco Pizarro and his brothers Gonzalo (c. 1502–48), Juan (c. 1511–c. 1536), and Hernando (c. 1508–c. 1578). After hearing stories of the wealth of the Inca Empire, Francisco led an expedition from present-day Panama to Peru in search of Incan gold. When he and his band of 106 infantry and 62 cavalry worked their way through the jungle and reached the Incan city of Cajamarca in 1532, Pizarro met with the Incan king Atahualpa. According to some accounts, a priest in Pizarro's party then stepped forward, handing Atahualpa a Bible and telling

him he must obey the great Christian God. Atahualpa flipped through the pages of the book but declared it made no sense to him. When the king threw it to the ground, the conquistadors opened fire, killing at least 2,000 Incas and taking 5,000 as captives, including Atahualpa.

Atahualpa made a deal with Pizzaro. He would give the conquistador leader a roomful of gold in exchange for his freedom. Hoping to rescue their king, the Incas gathered as much gold and silver as they could find. They even allowed the conquistadors to loot their sacred temples, graves, and shrines. But after the room was filled with gold, Pizarro ordered Atahaulpa's death, executing him by strangulation.

Pizarro became ruler of Peru, appointing a native named Manco Yupanqui as leader of the Incas. Manco was an ally of the Spaniards at first, but after a great deal of mistreatment at the hands of the Pizarro brothers, he led a rebellion against the Spaniards. Manco and the Incas fought valiantly, but defeat pushed them to Ollantaytambo, a town deep in the Andes Mountains. Hernando Pizarro pursued Manco, which led to the battle of Ollantaytambo. The Incas attacked the conquistador army from a set of high **terraces**, raining arrows and slinging boul-

FRANCISCO PIZZARO'S 1532 ENCOUNTER WITH ATAHUALPA SIGNALED THE BEGINNING OF THE END OF THE INCAS' EMPIRE

$\mathcal{T}$ales of a rumored Fountain of Youth swirled throughout the Spanish colonies in the early 1500s. According to legend, the fountain is a spring that restores the youth of anyone who drinks from it, effectively providing everlasting life. The legend had been popular among many cultures for thousands of years, and the indigenous people of the Caribbean also had beliefs about the fountain, which they said lay in Bimini, a mythical land to the north. When these rumors reached Spanish conquistador Juan Ponce de León (1474–1521) in 1513, he set off from Puerto Rico in search of the fountain. He explored present-day Florida but never found the fabled waters.

ders upon them until the Spanish retreated. It was the first Spanish defeat in the Americas. Gonzalo Pizarro, however, did not give up the chase. He led several campaigns against Manco, who retreated further into the Andes until he was finally discovered and killed, ending the Inca revolt.

Farther north, Francisco Vásquez de Coronado waged warring expeditions through what is now the American Southwest. While acting as governor of a region of northwestern Mexico, Coronado sent a party of four men led by friar Marcos de Niza (c. 1495–1558) in 1539 in search of the Seven Cities of Gold. When the friar returned with reports of a glittering city of gold called Cibola that he'd seen in the north, Coronado set off to find it. What followed was a haphazard journey through the American Southwest as Coronado, determined to find his gold, followed any lead given him by the natives he met. Coronado's party befriended some natives, such as the Teyas, and battled others, such as the Tiwa tribe along the Rio Grande. After nearly two years of wandering, Coronado returned to Mexico, defeated, and the fabled city of gold was never found.

One unusual conquistador was an African man named Estevanico. A Moroccan slave, he was brought to the Americas by conquistador Andres Dorantes (c. 1500–c. 1553), who included him on the ill-fated expedition of Pánfilo de Narváez (1478–1528). The Narváez expedition shipwrecked off the coast of present-day Florida in 1528, leaving only Estevanico and three other men as survivors. He traveled with his master and Álvar Nuñez Cabeza de Vaca (c. 1490–c. 1559) for eight years through Mexico and the American Southwest. Estevanico was skilled at learning languages and was able to converse with many natives. The conquistadors returned to Mexico, and in 1539, Estevanico was assigned to the expedition with Marcos de Niza in the search for Cibola. During that expedition, Estevanico was captured and killed by warriors of the Zuni tribe.

Francisco Pizarro (opposite) and other conquistadors had to learn to navigate mountains

THE CHANGED WORLD

As the conquistadors continued to conquer and colonize the New World, some Europeans began to ask whether the brutalities the Spaniards were committing were morally justified. Spain was a deeply Catholic country, and with the Christian religion came notions of morality and goodwill toward all people. However, many people still believed the native Americans were inferior to the Europeans, and the wealth they were enjoying because of the New World colonies was enough to compel leaders in Spain to look the other way. Many justified the wrongs by telling themselves they were saving the natives' souls by teaching them about Christianity.

A common question of the day was whether the Americans were human beings. Because their lifestyles and beliefs were so different from those of Europeans, people wondered if, in fact, the natives were actually part animal. Although this idea seems foolish today, for a long time it was common for members of some races to believe they were biologically superior to others. Still, some scholars spoke out against the mistreatment of the indigenous peoples, and in 1550, King Charles V of Spain (1500–58) gathered a council of 14 **philosophers, theologians,** and advisers to debate the issue. In the meantime, he ordered that all conquest expeditions be halted.

For one month in Valladolid, Spain, scholars on both sides of the issue presented their ideas to the king and his advisory council. Two of the most outspoken were Juan Ginés de Sepúlveda (1489–1573) and Bartolomé de Las Casas (c. 1474–1566). Sepúlveda argued that the differences between the natives and the Spanish were like the differences between apes and men and that the Spanish were justified in imposing their will. Sepúlveda, while a renowned thinker, had never set foot in the New World and had no personal observations to support his ideas. Las Casas,

SPANISH RULERS USED THE SPREAD OF CHRISTIANITY AS A REASON TO SUBDUE THE INCAS AND OTHER NATIVE AMERICANS

by contrast, was a Spanish priest who had spent many years in the Americas and witnessed the atrocities the conquistadors and colonists had committed. He argued that all the peoples of the world are human beings, formed by God in His own likeness. Las Casas ended on a powerful note: "Thus all humankind is one."

Although Las Casas's words struck a chord within the council, in the end, Charles V allowed the conquests to resume. He had decided, it seemed, that the wealth gained in the New World was too much to throw away upon a moralistic judgment. However, although Spain's colonization continued, the glory days of the conquistadors were over.

BARTOLOMÉ DE LAS CASAS WAS ONE OF THE FEW 16TH-CENTURY VOICES TO SPEAK AGAINST THE SPANIARDS' BRUTALITY

The Spanish conquistadors were the first Europeans to taste chocolate. Xocolatl *was a cold chocolate drink of the Aztecs and other indigenous people. It was made by mashing cacao seeds into a paste, then mixing in water, vanilla, chili peppers, cornmeal, and certain spices. The mixture was poured back and forth between two cups until it became a frothy, thick liquid. Because the natives often served xocolatl to their human sacrifices, the Spanish were frightened of it. They were also turned off by its bitter taste. When the Spanish began sweetening xocolatl with sugar, its popularity soared, and it became a favorite treat in Europe.*

CONQUISTADORS

After subduing and enslaving native populations, many conquistadors became rulers of their territory. However, their reign was often short-lived. Some fought wars against each other for domination of the area. The Pizarro brothers, for example, battled against another conquistador, Diego de Almagro (1475–1538), over control of Peru. The Pizarros were ultimately successful, but Francisco ended up being murdered by Almagro's son three years later. To control such volatile situations, Spain sent commissioners to replace many of the conquistador rulers.

Even after gaining wealth and land, many conquistadors were dissatisfied. They still yearned for gold, and even though El Dorado and Cibola were proving to be more myth than reality, many continued their quest for fortune. Cortés, after being removed from governorship in New Spain, launched more expeditions but never found the gold he was looking for. Like Christopher Columbus, Cortés died believing he was a failure.

Some conquistadors were put on trial for the brutal and unprovoked violence they brought against the natives, but very few were actually sentenced or punished. Coronado, for example, was acquitted on all charges of cruelty toward natives and was elected to serve in the government of New Spain. Some conquistadors made false accu-sations against each other out of jealousy. A rival Spaniard falsely accused Balboa of **treason** against Spain, alleging that Balboa was planning to take over the government near present-day Panama, and Balboa was publicly beheaded.

Many common soldiers of the conquistador armies remained in the Americas, abandoning their warring ways for lives in ranching, farming, or government. Some married native women and had children, forming the mixed ancestry characteristic of much of the population of Mexico and Central and South America today.

Colonization of the Americas continued until the entire New World was under European control. As the centuries wore on, colonists in the New World fought for independence from their European masters. By the early 20th century, all the colonies had become their own countries. Still, this independence came far too late to reclaim the indigenous cultures that were lost at the hands of the conquistadors.

In the centuries that followed the conquest of the New World, the conquistador became a heroic figure. Despite their wrongdoings, conquistadors were truly brave and ambitious men whose adventures inspired romantic ideas. Up until the 1900s, the story of the Spanish conquest was told primarily from a European point of view in

SAN FELIPE DEL MORRO, IN NORTHWESTERN PUERTO RICO, WAS THE FIRST SPANISH FORT BUILT IN THE NEW WORLD

schools and textbooks throughout Europe and the Americas. Only in the past century have the conquistadors been more broadly studied in a new light and their actions considered more barbaric than heroic.

The highly dramatic lives and deaths of the conquistadors have made them the subjects of novels, plays, and movies. Italian composer Lorenzo Ferrero depicts the Spanish conquest of Mexico in his 2005 opera *La Conquista*, a mixture of accounts from both the Europeans and the indigenous people, all told in their original languages. On the big screen, *The Captain from Castile* is a film released in 1947 that depicts a fictional warrior in Cortés's army. A 1998 Mexican film, *The Other Conquest*, tells of an Aztec man in 1520 Tenochtitlan after the Spanish conquered the city. On the comedic side, the 2000 animated movie *The Road to El Dorado* features fictional 16th-century Spanish con men who try to cheat their way to riches and end up in the kingdom of El Dorado, where they interact with the natives and try to steal as much gold as they can.

Although conquistadors no longer exist, their presence emanates throughout the Americas. Spanish architecture abounds on the two continents, and Christianity remains the predominant religion practiced. The Spanish language, as well, is the national language of Mexico and most Central and South American countries. But many native cultures that survived the conquest have revived old traditions in order to keep the memory of their ancestors alive. In the Andes, people of Incan descent continue to celebrate the Festival of the Sun, a ritual that predates the arrival of the Spanish conquerors.

Today, the legacy of the conquistadors remains mixed. Their conquest of the Americas changed the course of the world drastically but at a huge cost to the indigenous human population. No matter the perspective, it is certain that the Spaniards left their imprint upon the Americas. Under the sword of the conquistadors, a new world was born, and old ones were lost forever.

The Road to El Dorado features such historical characters as famed conquistador Hernán Cortés

*Machu Picchu is an Incan city in the mountains of Peru that went undiscovered and untouched by the conquistadors. Built around 1450 as an estate for an Incan emperor, the city, which sits 7,970 feet (2,430 m) above sea level, was discovered in 1911 by an American historian. Machu Picchu holds cultural and **archaeological** treasures and is often called "The Lost City of the Incas." The city contains nearly 200 homes and temples made of polished dry stone as well as numerous steps, fountains, and parks. Historians speculate that much of Machu Picchu's population was wiped out by smallpox in the 1500s.*

GLOSSARY

alliances—Agreements or unions between parties, specifically formed to further the interests of the members of each party or group

archaeological—Relating to the discovery or examination of relics of past human life; archaeological findings help explain the lives, activities, and customs of a culture

artillery—Large, powerful guns such as cannons that are mounted on wheels or tracks

banished—Ordered by authority to leave a place or country and not allowed to return either for a fixed amount of time or for the rest of one's life

cavalry—Soldiers who fight on horseback; historically, the most mobile of combat units

chain mail—A protective suit consisting of thousands of tiny metal loops linked meticulously together

colonizing—Establishing a new colony, or a territory settled by people from another country and controlled by that country

commodities—Economic goods; products that are bought and sold

empire—A major political unit or country that has wide-spread territory or a number of territories or peoples under a single authority

heathens—Members of a people or a nation who do not know about or worship the Christian God

heresy—Speaking against one's religion or religious rules, a charge often leveled by the Catholic Church during the Middle Ages (A.D. 476–1453)

hidalgo—A member of the lower nobility of Spain; unlike upper nobility, a hidalgo is usually not wealthy

indigenous—People living naturally in a particular region, or native to that region

infantry—Soldiers trained, armed, and equipped to fight on foot

literacy—The quality or state of being able to read and write

mestizos—A Spanish word describing people who have mixed European and native American ancestry

monarchs—People (usually kings or queens) who reign over a kingdom or empire; monarch rule is usually handed down within a royal family

Muslims—People who follow the religion of Islam, which upholds Allah as the sole God and Muhammad as a divine prophet; Muslims are most populous in areas of North Africa and the Middle East

nobleman—An important man who ranked high within society; often noblemen were wealthy, well-respected, and came from a long line of nobility

philosophers—People who study general and fundamental problems concerning truth, wisdom, and reason

rigging—The ropes and chains used aboard a sailing ship that support and control the sails; the term more broadly also describes the mast, yards, sails, and cordage

straits—Narrow channels connecting two larger bodies of water

terraces—Series of horizontal ridges made in a hillside to make the land flat for building or farming and to minimize erosion, or the wearing away of soil

theologians—People who study religious faith, practice, and experience; they seek to learn about God and God's relation to the world

treason—The crime of betraying or attempting to overthrow one's government

44

INDEX

BIBLIOGRAPHY

Descola, Jean. *The Conquistadors*. Translated by Malcolm Barnes. New York: Viking Press, 1957.

Horgan, Paul. *Conquistadors in North American History*. New York: Farrar, Straus, and Company, 1963.

Horwitz, Tony. *A Voyage Long and Strange: Rediscovering the New World*. New York: Henry Holt, 2008.

Innes, Hammond. *The Conquistadors*. New York: Alfred A. Knopf, 1969.

Pohl, John. *The Conquistador: 1492–1550*. New York: Osprey Publishing, 2001.

Wallace, David. *Conquistadors*. DVD. Arlington, Va.: PBS Home Video, 2006.

Wise, Terence. *The Conquistadors*. New York: Osprey Publishing, 1980.

Wood, Michael. *Conquistadors*. Los Angeles: University of California Press, 2000.